Deonte' Earl Towner
Pieces in the Dark

I want to change so bad, but this feeling will not go away. I want to make myself feel the way I make everyone else feel: worth it and loved.

-Deonte' Earl Towner

Every morning I wake up I remind myself that it's a new day, today is designed for a new start, and bad habits can be broken by the new choices that I make.

-Deonte' Earl Towner

My parents always taught me that I was worth it, but I never believed them because I kept falling in love with people that weren't worth it.

-Deonte' Earl Towner

Dear Self,

I am sorry for the pain I caused you. I am sorry for putting everyone else's needs before you.

-Deonte' Earl Towner

I'll never forget that night you called me and you were listening to all my stories about everyone that hurt me in the past. A few months later you ended up doing the same thing. You wrote me a long text explaining how you were sorry. It hurt me to the core because you promised me you wouldn't do me like that.

-Deonte' Earl Towner

Pieces in the Dark

Copyright © 2018 by Deonte Earl Towner

All rights reserved. This book or any portion thereof may not be reproduced or used in any manner whatsoever without the express written permission of the publisher except for the use of brief quotations in a book review.

Printed in the United States of America

First Printing, 2018

www.deontetowner.com

Dear my friend the reader,

This world can seem so dark and cold at times. Friends and family may not understand you at all. You maybe that friend that's there for everyone else, but it seems like no one is there for you. You may have made many mistakes in your past and the pain from those decisions may creep up sometimes. People may have walked out of your life and betrayed you. You may have had days where you wanted to say goodbye to life and distance yourself from everyone. Remember you are here for a reason. You may not be religious but remember God kept you alive for a reason. I tried committing suicide three times, but I realized that I have too much to offer this world. You don't realize how many people you can help with your story. Please don't give up. As you are reading the small passages related to times in my life I hope you feel less alone. Keep fighting until your victory is won.

Sincerely,

Pick up your new friend whenever you feel alone

Deonte'

Ps: Thanks mom and dad you are heaven sent. My dad is recovering from a stroke and my mom has been by my dad's side every day praying for his road to recovery.

(Emily & Joe Towner)

Thanks to my big sister Nina for always making me laugh during times that were meant to be serious. Thanks to my big brother Jojo for always freeing me in times I felt overwhelmed by the burdens of life.

Pieces in the Dark

You will find what you need in this book

Pieces in the Dark

Pieces in the Dark

Leonides Samantha "Amore" Hernandez
1993-2011

Pieces in the Dark

Pieces In The Dark

"Welcome to the secrets of my heart that I tried to hide from the world for years..."

Deonte' Earl Towner

Pieces in the Dark

On Monday…

I'm Good

The "I am good" response is the biggest lie of all time. Nobody is ever just good.

-Deonte' Earl Towner

Sometimes I tell myself mean things first so when other people say them it won't hurt as bad because I said it first.

-Deonte' Earl Towner

The worst part about experiencing a heart break is that nobody knows how much it physically and mentally hurts on the inside.

-Deonte' Earl Towner

My smile and loud laugh is my coping mechanism to hide all the pain within.

-Deonte' Earl Towner

It doesn't matter how many degrees you have, how popular your personality is, how much money you make a year… anyone can get played and cheated on. Don't allow your status in life to fool you.

-Deonte' Earl Towner

You can't make a person stay no matter how much love you offer them.

-Deonte' Earl Towner

It stings inside to know that you are using everything I taught you in your new relationship. I had to get hurt badly in order for you to reach your fullest potential. I wish you treated me like your new lover.

-Deonte' Earl Towner

Sometimes I feel like a caged bird.

You set me free, but then I came flying back to your captivity.

I have grown numb to the pain.

How can I give up now after I've given you my all?

-Deonte' Earl Towner

Be careful because sometimes people don't recover after they have hit rock bottom. Listen to the people that are trying to save you.

-Deonte' Earl Towner

Those times you tell everyone around you that you're single because you only want to focus on yourself, but deep down inside you feel lonely because you just want someone to love you as much as you loved them.

-Deonte' Earl Towner

The later I stay up the more I begin to think about all the people that walked out my life. My parents always told me that it was their loss, but those words of comfort don't take away the quiet sting I feel. I wish someone could hug my insides and tell me it's going to be alright until I fall asleep because counting sheep isn't working.

-Deonte' Earl Towner

Stuck between a rock and a hard place and I just want a soft place.

-Deonte' Earl Towner

I'll never forget the memories of me sitting in my sad blue colored wall room alone thinking no one understands me as a teenager.

-Deonte' Earl Towner

It sucks to know that a person can potentially become careless in how they treat you. What makes it worse is when your mind ponders off, and you begin to think about how they treated you in the beginning. They begin to slowly move on without realizing it. So you find yourself going with the flow waiting for the end and not realizing the end has already come.

-Deonte' Earl Towner

You can't look at someone and determine if they are happy or not. Some people have been wearing a mask for years.

-Deonte' Earl Towner

Sometimes I know what people are thinking about me when I walk into a room. It use to hurt, but now I do not care. I accept all of me.

-Deonte' Earl Towner

I will never forget the day when my parents were driving all the way to Florida. I was in the back seat crying the whole ride through Texas because I realized that all my efforts weren't good enough. I tried so hard at the age of 17 to make you love me.

-Deonte' Earl Towner

I want to change so bad, but this feeling will not go away. I want to make myself feel the way I make everyone else feel: worth it and loved.

-Deonte' Earl Towner

Growing up my parents would always say, "You know better."

That voice carried in my head every time I committed a mistake in my adulthood.

-Deonte' Earl Towner

Every morning I wake up I remind myself that it's a new day and today is designed for a new start, and bad habits can be broken by the new choices that I make.

-Deonte' Earl Towner

During the day I feel great, but then at night I feel lonely inside.

-Deonte' Earl Towner

I was right about you all along. It makes me angry because I allowed you in. I should have listened to my gut feeling. You can't love unless you take chances and me giving you this chance ended like every other relationship. I am trying to keep the hope alive, but it seems like this hope is killing me on the inside.

-Deonte' Earl Towner

I'm tired of people only running to me when they need advice because when everything is going fine in their life they leave me… I am tired of getting left.

-Deonte' Earl Towner

You have the power to change the world don't let the world change you.

-Phone conversations with my mother

You're only hurting yourself when you hurt others.

-Deonte' Earl Towner

When people get too close to me I tend to distance myself because I am afraid they won't like the real me.

-Deonte' Earl Towner

Success isn't measured by how much money you make but by how much love you gave.

-Phone conversations with my mother

Sometimes your closes friends switch up first.

-Deonte' Earl Towner

I honestly can't believe you made me feel this way after you told me every single day that you loved me.

-Deonte' Earl Towner

Life is worth living no matter how sad it is.

-Deonte' Earl Towner

I left everything I was taught, left behind everyone I loved just to be with you and now you want to walk away from me?

-Deonte' Earl Towner

Learning that I don't have to respond to everything.

-Deonte' Earl Towner

Sometimes we bash things in public that we privately do behind closed doors.

-Deonte' Earl Towner

Sometimes we portray ourselves to be stronger than what we are.

-Deonte' Earl Towner

Everyone in life makes mistakes.

You can't cut everyone off that hurts you because you'll find yourself alone not able to turn to anyone when you make a mistake.

-Deonte' Earl Towner

Stay away from people that can't make their own decisions.

-Deonte' Earl Towner

Hanging out with people that have no goals is dangerous.

-Deonte' Earl Towner

Allow me to be myself without judging me for living in my truth.

-Deonte' Earl Towner

I've done things that I don't even want myself to know about.

-Deonte' Earl Towner

I try my hardest to refocus when I find myself slipping back into my old ways.

-Deonte' Earl Towner

There's nothing worse than not being able to trust yourself anymore.

-Deonte' Earl Towner

When I was a child my parents would shelter me from the world, but then as I got older I realized the world isn't so kind after all.

I often lay in bed wishing that my eyes were still protected from mother earth.

-Deonte' Earl Towner

There are nights I whisper to myself in bed saying "I don't want to live like this anymore."

-Deonte' Earl Towner

It hurts to know that whenever I walk into a room I already know what they are thinking about. That misjudgment is something I am going to have to live with for the rest of my life and it took me some years to be at peace with that. I've learned to use misconceptions as a time to educate others.

-Deonte' Earl Towner

Your parents treated you like royalty. Your parents called you their little prince or princess. Your parents told you they loved you every second of the day… but the person you fell in love with degrades and exploits who you are.

-Deonte' Earl Towner

On Tuesday…

I'm Worth It

Be careful how you treat me because I may just wake up one day, realize my worth, walk away and never come back.
-Deonte' Earl Towner

Sometimes the person that preaches to others about self-worth is the main one that has no worth and secretly allows others to abuse their boundaries.

-Deonte' Earl Towner

When a person leaves your life don't cry, don't stress and don't reach out to them. Remember it's their loss not yours.

-Deonte' Earl Towner

Things begin to change when you realize your worth.

-Phone conversations with my mother

You'll stop getting hurt so much when you begin to understand not everyone deserves your time and energy.

-Deonte' Earl Towner

Learning to protect my heart because I have been giving it away to people that don't deserve it.

-Deonte' Earl Towner

I'm afraid that if I become too demanding and create boundaries then you will walk away from me and decide to be with someone else.

-Deonte' Earl Towner

Stop allowing yourself to fall for sweet words so easily.

-Deonte' Earl Towner

My parents taught me to never allow anyone to disrespect me… but I never thought that I would allow someone to degrade me years later and make excuses for their behavior.

-Deonte' Earl Towner

I know I am worth it but why do I keep allowing myself to fall into these predicaments. No one would ever look at me and think I would allow another human being to treat me this way.

-Deonte' Earl Towner

Keep your head up my grandmother always told me. I love you and that should be enough.

-Deonte' Earl Towner

You can't make anyone see or understand your worth.

-Deonte' Earl Towner

Stop wasting your time trying to make people understand you.

-Deonte' Earl Towner

No matter how much love you received growing up no one can make you feel worth it. Worth is something that you discover on the inside.

-Deonte' Earl Towner

My parents always taught me that I was worth it, but I never believed them because I kept falling in love with people that weren't worth it.

-Deonte' Earl Towner

I try my hardest to look like I am over you and that I am happier without you on my social media accounts. Deep down inside I am frowning because I miss you. Whenever I feel like reaching out to you I have to remind myself that I am worth it. You don't deserve my time or attention anymore.

-Deonte' Earl Towner

On Wednesday…

I'm Questioning Everything

What would my heart say if it could talk? Would it be mad at me? Would it yell at me? Would it give me words of advice? Would it ask to live in someone else's body? Would it be proud of me? Would it think I am strong like everyone else thinks I am? Would it rip me to shreds for causing it so much pain? Would it have mercy on me and forgive me? Would it sing a sad song about all the battles it had to fight within me? Will it sing a song about joy? Or, will it walk away ashamed and defeated? Would it look into my eyes and make me cry?

-Deonte' Earl Towner

Why do I keep allowing you to hurt me? Why don't I walk away and leave? Do I find joy in how you hurt me? Will this ever end? Or, do I have to wait for you to walk away because I am not strong enough to leave? Can you please make it easier for me and walk away from me first? Because I do not have the strength to walk away from you.

-Deonte' Earl Towner

What if I go through my whole life never thinking I'm good enough? Will I ever feel fulfilled?

-Deonte' Earl Towner

When will the nights stop where I lay deep in my covers sad over someone that hurt me?

-Deonte' Earl Towner

Our parents always tell us as children to be ourselves and do what makes us happy, but what if who we really want to be isn't pleasing to their eyes?

-Deonte' Earl Towner

Why did you go back on your word?

-Deonte' Earl Towner

Are you going to give up on us when you get bored with me?

-Deonte' Earl Towner

What if it doesn't get easier?

What if I have to live with this for the rest of my life?

-Deonte' Earl Towner

Where were you when I needed you? Every time you needed me I was always there.

-Deonte' Earl Towner

What if it doesn't get better?

What if it's not alright?

-Deonte' Earl Towner

Why are you treating me like I am the one that did this? You broke my heart.

-Deonte' Earl Towner

What is the solution to all my problems?

-Deonte' Earl Towner

Why don't I create boundaries with people?
Why do I accept anything from people that I give my all to?
Why do I complain about the same thing but do nothing about it?
Am I scared for them to walk away and not come back?
-Deonte' Earl Towner

How can you say that we aren't made for each other after all that we have invested in each other?

-Deonte' Earl Towner

What if I fail? What If I never fulfill my goals in life? What if everything comes crashing and burning? What if I make a fool out of myself?

-Deonte' Earl Towner

Will I ever move on from the mistakes that I made?
How can I ever forgive myself?
What if everyone finds out?
My reputation will be ruined and no one will ever see me the same.

-Deonte' Earl Towner

What if I shame my families name?
What if I don't stick to everything they taught me?

-Deonte' Earl Towner

What if I leave and never comeback?
What If I decide to walk away and I never find anyone better?
Should I settle or pray for things to change?

-Deonte' Earl Towner

Are we too close to call this a friendship?

-Deonte' Earl Towner

Why couldn't you tell me the truth from the beginning?
Why did you have to lie the whole time?
Were you trying to protect my feelings?
Were you playing me all along?
What part was true?
Or was everything a lie to you?

-Deonte' Earl Towner

Did I love you too much?
Did I love you too hard?
Was it my fault?
Was I too good to you?

-Deonte' Earl Towner

What can I do to make you stay? I have tried everything. I have even hurt myself emotionally trying to please you. My parents taught me to go after what I want and I guess that didn't work when it came to you and I.

-Deonte' Earl Towner

Would I have listened if I could go back in time and give my younger self advice on love? Or, would I act like I know everything?

-Deonte' Earl Towner

What am I teaching you by allowing you to come into my life after you hurt me? Are you beginning to lose respect for me? Are you beginning to see that no matter how much you hurt me I will always let you back in?

-Deonte' Earl Towner

Am I good enough?

-Deonte' Earl Towner

What do you do when you get tired of everything?

-Deonte' Earl Towner

Why can't I see the greatness inside of me that others see?

-Deonte' Earl Towner

Will who I really am begin to catch up to me? Will anyone ever see the real me?

-Deonte' Earl Towner

Why did I not walk away when I felt you distancing yourself from me?

-Deonte' Earl Towner

Have you ever had one of those relationships where you couldn't get them out of your head?

-Deonte' Earl Towner

Why did you hurt me after you promised me that you weren't like everyone else in my past?

-Deonte' Earl Towner

Is it possible to grow up in a loving family but not love yourself?

-Deonte' Earl Towner

What do you do when the person you love is becoming careless in how they treat you but your mind won't let go because it keeps reminding you of how they first started off?

-Deonte' Earl Towner

How many times am I going to keep falling for the same things?

-Deonte' Earl Towner

How did we get to this point?

-Deonte' Earl Towner

Can you force things to go back to how they use to be?

-Deonte' Earl Towner

Can you stop someone from distancing themselves from you?

-Deonte' Earl Towner

How much more can I take before I fall back into my old habits?

-Deonte' Earl Towner

Pieces in the Dark

On Thursday…

I'm Sorry You Said To Me…

The more you say I am sorry, the less meaningful it is. You can't keep apologizing and expecting everything to go back to how it was.

- I'm sorry D

I'm sorry for hurting you… I don't understand why I keep doing it. I hope you believe that I love you. Please don't think I love you any less because I keep hurting you.

-I'm sorry D

I'm sorry for all the pain that I caused you to feel deep down inside. I'm supposed to be the one that makes you feel good not worse. Please forgive me. This is the last time I do that. I have learned my lesson I promise.

- I'm sorry D

Be careful of your actions and the things you say because you can't take it back with a sorry or an "I didn't mean it like that…" things may never be the same again and you can lose a real one that only wanted to love and be there for you… that's rare to find.

-Deonte' Earl Towner

You were the best thing that has ever come into my life. I do not get why I keep pushing you away. I know that I will never be able to replace you, but I understand if you never want to give me another chance. I love you and I am sorry. I also understand if you never reply again. Just know that you will always be in my heart. Everything you have taught me will always remain. You are a good person and you don't deserve all the hurt that I am causing you. Whenever I need advice I won't reach out to you. Instead I will think about everything you would say to me and find comfort in that.

- I'm sorry D

Dear Self,

I am sorry for the pain I caused you. I am sorry for putting everyone else's needs before you.

-Deonte' Earl Towner

I'll never forget that night you called me and you were listening to all my stories about everyone that hurt me in the past. A few months later you ended up doing the same thing. You wrote me a long text explaining how you were sorry. It hurt me to the core because you promised me you wouldn't do me like that.

- I'm sorry D

Every time you see me in public you hug me softly and tell me you are sorry for everything.

- I'm sorry D

As I cried you kept apologizing, but it saddened me even more because your apologies didn't make it better like they did before and at that moment is when I realized that there was nothing else to give.

- I'm sorry D

I'm not in love with you like I was before. Every time you think about reaching out to me, every time you think of my name, eveytime you need advice think about what I would say. I will always live inside your heart but just not in your life. I'm sorry but I have to move on.

- I'm sorry D

You are not sorry for what you did you are only sorry because I am finally strong enough to leave. In all actuality it is not your fault because I allowed you to treat me this way. I apologize to you for making you think it was ok. Lastly, I apologize to myself for making myself suffer through the pain. Maybe I didn't think I deserved true love. That's why I always settle for less. I really need to stop getting myself in these same perdicimites.

-Deonte' Earl Towner

When I was crying you said I am sorry for hurting you. You deserve someone better. But you don't understand because all I want is you. I want it to work, but I know that you will never change and I will only suffer.

-Deonte' Earl Towner

You loved them the way that I stressed to be loved by you. What did they do that I didn't do? What did they give you that I didn't give?

-Deonte' Earl Towner

I'm sorry that I couldn't be everything that I promised to you in the beginning.

- I'm sorry D

I'm sorry but I am going to accept this last apology then move on.

-Deonte' Earl Towner

Pieces in the Dark

Whenever you get lonely think of me. We have enough memories to keep each other alive in our hearts. Please don't think of the times I did you wrong. Only think about the good times in the summer. I am so sorry for the way hings ended. Everything has its season and our time is up. We have to move on and find love with someone else. I know that you are crying reading this but no matter how much I say sorry I keep doing the same things to you. I am going to do your heart justice by walking away instead of lying and promising you that I will change. Just because our love didn't last doesn't mean that it wasn't real.

- I'm sorry D

I love you too much to keep allowing myself to hurt you. You are a good person, and I know the more I hurt you the more you want to hurt yourself. You love me so much you blame yourself for how I treat you. I am sorry but I can't continue this relationship with you. Love isn't about taking advantage of the person you love and I am doing that to you.

- I'm sorry D

On Friday…

I'm Moving On

When you've moved on from someone you are not constantly asking yourself anymore, "Do they miss me? Are they thinking of me? Do they feel hurt because they do not have me around anymore?" Those thoughts don't come to your mind anymore…"

-Deonte' Earl Towner

No longer getting sad at night when I randomly think of you.

-Deonte' Earl Towner

I began to move on when I realized that I wasn't losing anything by letting you go. If anything I was losing all the pain that you were causing me and replacing it with the joy by doing myself the favor of letting you go.

-Deonte' Earl Towner

You love me but you didn't love me enough to stop cheating.

-Deonte' Earl Towner

I need you to help me move on from you. I have never been heartbroken but I know you have. Can you please show me all the ways you moved on from your exes so I can use everything you learned to use for our situation?

-Deonte' Earl Towner

I don't care how sick I was my mom would whisper to me and say that I am going to get better. That's the same voice that comes into my head when I am trying my hardest to move on from somebody. That's the only hope I have is her voice.

-Deonte' Earl Towner

I woke up one morning and realized that you don't have power over my mind anymore.

-Deonte' Earl Towner

I broke down and begged for the truth because I was sensing that you were distancing yourself from me. The truth was that you loved me but you were tired of trying to work things out. I didn't want to give up but you told me when something isn't working you have to move on because somethings can't be repaired when it's been broken multiple times.

-Deonte' Earl Towner

Please let me move on in peace. If I call you please do not answer. If I try to text you please do not respond. Please help me stay strong. I am trying my hardest to distance myself from you.

-Deonte' Earl Towner

My parents taught me better. I know better. What am I doing? I can't give you anymore of me. I look in the mirror and I don't know who I am anymore. Love isn't supposed to make you feel like this. Sometimes I cry in my dark room because I have forsaken everything that my parents have taught me in order to please you.

-Deonte' Earl Towner

If you have to keep telling yourself, you've moved on and you're over it… most likely you're not.

-Deonte' Earl Towner

I can't be mad at you for hurting me. I only have myself to be mad at because I saw all the warning signs before you hurt me, but I decided to ignore them because I had so much faith in you that you would change. I have no choice but to move on because you don't want anything to do with me and there's nothing else left.

-Deonte' Earl Towner

Never allow anyone to put a time limit on how long it should take you to move on. Moving on is an art. You mourn, laugh and pretend to be completely fine without them until you reach that point of forgiving them and yourself.

-Deonte' Earl Towner

I've learned how to move on without looking back.

-Deonte' Earl Towner

Moving on is hard especially when you can't sleep at night and your mind keeps going back to the first time you met.

-Deonte' Earl Towner

Sometimes I sit and cry whenever someone brings your name up or when I see something that reminds me of you… we were so sure of our future everything about the present makes me cry.

-Deonte' Earl Towner

No matter how hard you try… you can't be close to someone that doesn't want you.

-Deonte' Earl Towner

Sometimes you have to distance yourself from the ones you love in order to find yourself again.

-Deonte' Earl Towner

Every day we are moving on from something or someone.

-Deonte' Earl Towner

In life we make choices. We either choose to be sad or happy. You are in control of how you feel.

-Phone conversations with my mother

Pieces in the Dark

On Saturday…

I'm In LOVE

I can't stop myself from falling. All those walls I have created are beginning to tumble down. I am scared, but I have to give love a try. I have guarded myself too long. it's time to take a risk.

-Deonte' Earl Towner

For years I have been searching for that home feeling. I am so grateful to have found it in your love. When I am with you the world stops, everything comes to a halt, and nothing else around me seems to matter but you.

-Deonte' Earl Towner

People that fall in love too easily tend to get their hearts broken a lot. Those people have the saddest stories if you take the time to listen to them, but at first glance they look carefree, happy, free spirited, but deep down inside they are empty and sad.

-Deonte' Earl Towner

I promise that I won't allow anything from my past to hinder me from our love advancing. I promise not to punish you for the faults of my exes. I promise that I have moved on and have put all that into the past. I am ready to give you all of me.

-Deonte' Earl Towner

Loving someone that's willing to put in all the effort you are putting in is the greatest gift in life.

-Deonte' Earl Towner

Make sure you are able to love yourself and others after the relationship is over. Don't allow anyone to take the gift of love away from you.

-Deonte' Earl Towner

It's easier to believe other people outside of our relationship because you've messed up so many times in the past.

-Deonte' Earl Towner

It's time for me to start over and begin to love myself again. Giving my love and energy to others isn't working out so well.

-Deonte' Earl Towner

I let this person in.

-Deonte' Earl Towner

Sometimes we don't realize how much a person loved us until years later.

-Deonte' Earl Towner

You sucked all the love out of me and left me on the floor sobbing with nothing else to offer another soul.

-Deonte' Earl Towner

Run when a person promises to be your everything…

-Deonte' Earl Towner

I want your love to fill that hole inside my heart that I have constantly felt growing up.

-Deonte' Earl Towner

I fall in love too easily because sweet words always win me over.

-Deonte' Earl Towner

Sometimes I cry when I think about my first time in love because during that time I was innocent, unguarded and I thought people loved like my parents loved me. I thought that everyone's definition of love was the same. I was able to give the person my all without questioning them of hurting me in the future. I cry a lot when I think about you because I will never feel the amount of freedom as I did when I first fell in love with you. From now on I will always be guarded.

-Deonte' Earl Towner

Sometimes you love someone so much you begin to make excuses for all the reasons why they aren't loving you like they promised.

-Deonte' Earl Towner

I'm scared because the deeper I fall in love with you the less I know who I am. My identity is lost in you, and if you leave then I have nothing. I am willing to do whatever it takes to make us last.

-Deonte' Earl Towner

I am becoming so much in love with myself that it's hard to want anyone else.

-Deonte' Earl Towner

Be grateful for your relationship because someone out there is waiting for them.

-Deonte' Earl Towner

Liars love to swear on everything they love.

-Deonte' Earl Towner

I'm in love with someone that I already know is going to betray me. I already see the warning signs, but I am trying my hardest to love you hard so we can beat the odds.

-Deonte' Earl Towner

When you are single you wish that you were in a relationship because you don't want to be alone, but no one ever told me that you can feel lonely in a relationship.

-Deonte' Earl Towner

Nothing worse than realizing that you love and care about them more than they love you.

-Deonte' Earl Towner

My biggest mistake was thinking I could train someone how to love me but what I required from them wasn't in their nature.

-Deonte' Earl Towner

Most of the time I tell others to know your worth and stop falling in love too easily, but behind the scenes I end up falling in love too fast, lower my standards and end up getting hurt. In everyone else's mind I am a superhero, but on the inside I am a sad soul trying to find love like everyone else.

-Deonte' Earl Towner

It's not safe to fall in love with someone that's confused because one day they may decide that everything they said to you was a mistake.

-Deonte' Earl Towner

It's sad when two people fall in love then months or years later they realize that there's nothing that's keeping them in the relationship anymore.

-Deonte' Earl Towner

Our relationship is starting to feel like I am climbing a never ending mountain: unable to reach the top.

-Deonte' Earl Towner

When you're single you want to be in a relationship, and when you are in a relationship you want to be single. Nobody is ever satisfied in life.

-Deonte' Earl Towner

Everything was going good until I realized you didn't feel the same way. It all started off with the "Can I be honest and tell you how I feel." After you told me how you felt I was more crushed than ever on the inside because I let you in so easily.

-Deonte' Earl Towner

Pieces in the Dark

On Sunday…

I'm learning

I'm learning that life will keep throwing the same type of person at you until you choose to walk away and fall in love with something different.

-Deonte' Earl Towner

I'm learning not to explain myself to people because they will never understand who I am and where I am coming from.

-Deonte' Earl Towner

I'm learning that growing up with someone doesn't necessarily translate to loyalty.

-Deonte' Earl Towner

I'm learning that some people go through hell every day.

-Deonte' Earl Towner

I'm learning to use "no" as a complete sentence.

-Deonte' Earl Towner

I'm learning that I can't keep complaining about how people treat me if I keep allowing it time after time.

-Deonte' Earl Towner

I'm learning to set boundaries with people that I love because if I don't then their passions and desires will take over our relationship and when I get uncomfortable with how things are it will be too late to change everything because I have made their behavior in our relationship the norm by not stopping it a long time ago.

-Deonte' Earl Towner

I'm learning that a person doesn't have to say it's over to know that it's over.

-Deonte' Earl Towner

I'm learning that life is what I truly make it. All hell can be going on around me but I choose to see the good in what is in front of me. Life is constantly changing and I have to always be ready to find my new happy.

-Deonte' Earl Towner

I'm learning that in order to be successful then you must be able to adapt to the changes around you.

-Deonte' Earl Towner

I'm learning that in times of sorrow it's important to do the things that bring you joy.

-Deonte' Earl Towner

Pieces in the Dark

I'm learning that depression is racing behind me and it's trying to stop the sunshine from shinning in my life, but I won't let it catch up to me.

-Deonte' Earl Towner

I'm learning that I am stronger than I think and that scares me.

-Deonte' Earl Towner

I'm learning that I am not perfect and no matter how high my title is in life I am still human.

-Deonte' Earl Towner

I'm learning that nobody can make life worth it but myself.

-Deonte' Earl Towner

I'm learning that there's a difference between people that I have fun with and people I call friends.

-Deonte' Earl Towner

I'm learning to count my blessings until my troubles look smaller.

-Deonte' Earl Towner

I'm learning that I didn't stop judging people until I began living on my own, experiencing life and making my own mistakes.

-Deonte' Earl Towner

I'm learning that people make their lives look better than it actually is on social media.

-Deonte' Earl Towner

I'm learning that I can run on longer than I think I can.

-Deonte' Earl Towner

I'm learning that everyone starts off nice.

-Deonte' Earl Towner

I'm learning that I set myself up to get hurt when I make myself overly available to people.

-Deonte' Earl Towner

I'm learning how to defeat the enemy in battle.

-Phone conversations with my mom

I'm learning that we have to watch what we say to people because you never know how low they are already feeling on the inside.

-Deonte' Earl Towner

I'm learning that there are somethings I will never forget and I have to be able to make peace with myself, so whenever the thought comes up it doesn't affect me anymore.

-Deonte' Earl Towner

I'm learning that when I am not honest with myself then I cannot be honest with other people and if I can't be honest with myself or other people then I am living a lie.

-Deonte' Earl Towner

I'm learning that there is nothing wrong with going to places alone. Sometimes you get more done.

-Deonte' Earl Towner

I'm learning that it's not good to keep popping in and out of someone's life. Either you're going to stay for good or leave them alone forever.

-Deonte' Earl Towner

I'm learning that I will never find everything in one person.

-Deonte' Earl Towner

I'm learning that I need to set clear boundaries.

-Deonte' Earl Towner

I'm learning that my needs matter in a relationship.

-Deonte' Earl Towner

I'm learning the older we get the less we put up with things.

-Deonte' Earl Towner

I'm learning that everything that I went through was for my good.

-Deonte' Earl Towner

I'm learning that there's a difference between making someone a priority and actually being one to them.

-Deonte' Earl Towner

I'm learning the fire won't stop until you pour water on it.

-Deonte' Earl Towner

I'm learning that it's not always wise to cut off someone that hurt you because they can be useful in the future when you need a favor.

-Deonte' Earl Towner

I'm learning that everyone has their own definition of love and in order for it to work out then we have to come to an agreement on what it's going to mean between us.

-Deonte' Earl Towner

I'm learning that some people learn from experience and others learn from observation.

-Deonte' Earl Towner

I'm learning that you can't stop a person from distancing themselves.

-Deonte' Earl Towner

I'm learning that I wanted you to be me in my life more than you wanted to be in it.

-Deonte' Earl Towner

I'm learning that I don't have to search for home in other people because home already lives inside of me.

-Deonte' Earl Towner

I'm learning that I am more than enough.

-Deonte' Earl Towner

I'm learning that nobody else can give me freedom.

-Deonte' Earl Towner

I'm learning that it is perfectly fine to slow down.

-Deonte' Earl Towner

I'm learning that I pretend to be tough but inside I am a big softy.

-Deonte' Earl Towner

I'm learning to be careful who I make my world so fast.

-Deonte' Earl Towner

I'm learning that human nature isn't as kind as it was towards me when I was a little child. The older I get the more wicked it becomes.

-Deonte' Earl Towner

I'm learning to enjoy my nights alone.

-Deonte' Earl Towner

I'm learning that no matter how old I get my parents will always treat me like their baby. I am perfectly fine with that because they will not be on this earth forever, and I need to cherish the moments they make me feel like a kid again because once they are gone I will never be able to get that feeling back.

-Deonte' Earl Towner

I'm learning to love the way I act and not worry so much about how people perceive me. How they perceive me is their problem and not mine. I have made peace within and accepted things that are out of my control. I choose freedom and what you choose is your choice.

-Deonte' Earl Towner

I'm learning that everything doesn't deserve a response.

-Deonte' Earl Towner

I'm learning that it's not my job to help save everyone.

-Deonte' Earl Towner

I'm learning that it's important to forgive ourselves.

-Deonte' Earl Towner

I'm learning that all of my accomplishments won't stop a person from trying to play games with my heart.

-Deonte' Earl Towner

I'm learning that it's impossible to reach everyone.

-Deonte' Earl Towner

Pieces in the Dark

I'm learning that the best way to help ME is to stop replying and to leave them alone.

-Deonte' Earl Towner

I'm learning that I can't stop loving people just because others have hurt me in the past.

-Deonte' Earl Towner

I'm learning that everyone isn't the same.

-Deonte' Earl Towner

I'm learning that I can be strong on my own.

-Deonte' Earl Towner

I'm learning to look at things for what they are instead of what I want them to be.

-Deonte' Earl Towner

I'm learning that my parents tried their hardest to shelter me from everything that I went through. Everything that I went through was for my good, and if I didn't go through it I wouldn't of been able to write this book. It was all a blessing in disguise.

-Deonte' Earl Towner

Pieces in the Dark

www.ingramcontent.com/pod-product-compliance
Lightning Source LLC
Chambersburg PA
CBHW070141100426
42743CB00013B/2788